MAKE THE Bible WORK FOR YOU

 REVEREND HELLENBACK

with Dave Johnston

ABRAMS IMAGE

NEW YORK

To whom righteousness concerns,

As a man of God and a confidant of the Almighty, it weighs heavily upon me that the subject that most vexes our Lord—after pestilence, war, and where platypuses came from—is how badly the Good Book has been misinterpreted by those who claim true Knowledge. I confess that sometimes when my fellow Christians tell me of all the things the Bible says they cannot do, I wonder what book they've been reading. With God as my Witness, if I believed half of what they told me about what I could eat, dinosaurs, or whom I could not have relations with, I'd be hopping around the forest in druid robes or praying to some sort of giant snake creature. Truly, why would anyone join a religion if they were not going to get any pleasure out of it? Believe me when I say that if the Lord did not wish humanity to be happy, He would not have invented whiskey, curly fries, and half-price tickets to the water park.

This schism among Believers as to what the Bible truly means is why I've decided to organize some of my thoughts into the tome that thou currently hold in thine hands, thus clearing up any confusion about the Good Book forever. The Bible encourages us all to go out and enjoy life. As a matter of fact, in my opinion the only real rules in the Good Book are the Ten Commandments, and they constitute what I refer to as firm suggestions. Certainly, killing is and will almost always be a sin. But coveting thy neighbor's wife? Lord give me strength. If the Almighty did not want me to covet my neighbor's wife just a little bit, he would not have let Ron and Bev Liebman and Bev's freckled cleavage move in next door to me.

This book contains just a small sampling of the behavior that is considered acceptable by both the Old Testament and the don't-let-it-fool-thee, almost-as-old New Testament. If thou wants to send an enemy to prison for a crime they did not commit or to marry thy cocker spaniel, look it up: I'm sure it is in there as well.

Thy devout servant,

the Reverend Hellenback

Be not righteous over much.
(Ecclesiastes 7:16)

Being thirty-two years old and going to thy girlfriend's senior prom

---

Let no man despise thy youth.

(1 Timothy 4:12)

Are we to question the Lord just because some of His comeliest creations are members of their school's field hockey team and wear braces? The inner light of the young, along with their overall firmness, is to be treasured, not reviled. Embrace thy intergenerational romance by finding interests that ye share, such as video games and teenagers. Reject those who would belittle thee, for this is just jealousy over thy nomination for prom king. However, whatever thou dost, beware the father of thy beloved, because he is just going to kill thee.

Wearing an "I'm with stupid" T-shirt to thy son's college visit

<hr>

And one of the multitude answered and said, Master, I have brought unto thee my son, which hath a dumb spirit.

(Mark 9:17)

<hr>

Take this to thy heart: Thou art not going to fool any college, as they've already seen thy child's test scores. And even if they haven't, once thy child opens his mouth, the truth will come dribbling out in mispronounced sentence fragments. Admit the truth with a smile on thy face and suggest that maybe thy child can be the anchor who holds down the wrong end of the bell curve. As for thy child, hopefully thou hast exposed him to these sorts of lessons throughout his childhood, because in the marathon of life he will perpetually be handing out water bottles.

Eating thy seatmate's forearm after a plane crash in the Andes

*The fool foldeth his hands together,
and eateth his own flesh.*

(Ecclesiastes 4:5)

There are those souls who refuse to eat their fellow man in case of emergency and there is also a name for them: "hors d'oeuvres." If thy plane crashes, thy yacht runs aground on a island, or thou art stuck on the median with a flat tire, recognize that the flesh of thine companions is an available and somewhat palatable source of nourishment. Know this: If the Lord did not want thee eating other people, then He would not have made them of meat. The subject of cannibalism is a sensitive one; when thou bringest up the idea with thy companions, be gentle but firm on the idea that someone must eventually be eaten. To take thyself off the day's menu, drop to one knee, touch the side of thy nose, and yell, "Not it!"

Ingratiating thyself to others with a series of nicknames and gratuitous high fives

---

*And Nathan said to David,
Thou art the man.*

(2 Samuel 12:7)

One way to create fellowship with thy workmates is to reach out to them by making up clever nicknames for them. How art thou to come up with such catchy endearments? Pick a defining physical characteristic of an officemate and make light of it. Also, try to make them feel as if they are the center of the universe as they walk into a room, by shouting, "Look out! Here comes trouble!" Other endearing mannerisms certain to warm the hearts of others? Punching knuckles, high fives, quick-draw six-shooter fingers, and endlessly repeating catchphrases thou heard on television.

Explaining to the arresting officers that thou art not under their jurisdiction

---

*But if ye be led of the Spirit,
ye are not under the law.*

(Galatians 5:18)

Earthly authorities must come to terms with the fact that thou art judged by higher laws than theirs. Thy directions come directly from the Almighty, who has taught thee to do as thou wishes, for it pleases Him. So if thou choose to attack a statue with a tree branch, then no officer of the law should detain thee, or require that thou put some clothes on whilst speaking to them. Remember that while they might shackle thy wrists and ankles, and pepper-spray thee repeatedly, they can never imprison thy Spirit.

Applying cologne as
if it were sunscreen

*Because of the savour of thy good
ointments thy name is as ointment poured
forth, therefore do the virgins love thee.*

(Song of Solomon 1:3)

If there is one thing that television and the Bible have taught us, it is the immense power of men's cologne. Truly, women are helpless in the face of odors derived from oil, gasoline, and—not to forget the scent that wields the greatest power over them—musk. As in all things, if a little works, a lot will work better. Therefore refresh thyself with the scent of thy choice, as would a bird that splashes about in a birdbath or a dog that rolls excitedly in excrement. When tears come to thine eyes, thou hast reached the correct Godly amount. Simply await the unending parade of virginesque women who will undoubtedly approacheth from downwind.

Helping thy friend obtain early release from jail with thy pickup truck and twenty feet of chain

For now will I break his yoke from off thee, and will burst thy bonds in sunder.

(Nahum 1:13)

Only the Almighty truly stands in judgment, despite what thine imprisoned associate might have been told by a jury of his peers. That said, the Lord is full of forgiveness and there is no spiritual satisfaction for those who are incarcerated. If thine associate feels even the littlest bit of remorse over the pain of his victim or simply regret at getting caught, then that is good enough for the Lord. As for thine involvement, the wheels of earthly justice are slow but the wheels of thy pickup are fast and full of torque, so thou shouldst have no problem with the bars.

Alarming neighbors with thy loud bedroom vocalizations

Lord, all my desire is before thee; and my groaning is not hid from thee.

(Psalms 38:9)

It is only natural for thee to praise the actions of thy bedfellow, whether by yelling their name or God's name in Spanish or any colorful language reflecting upon the actions that thou art partaking in currently. The Bible teaches that being vocal is a way to display thine increasing levels of satisfaction or to alert thy partner to chafing. As for neighbors and their broomsticks, the fact that they cannot find any pleasure in thy pleasure is just sinful.

Auctioning off the internal organs of strangers on the Internet

---

And the two kidneys, and the fat that is on them, which is by the flanks, and the caul above the liver, with the kidneys, it shall he take away.

(Leviticus 3:4)

Blessed be thou for the service that thou art performing for those who are both sickly and affluent. Some might question how thou came across so many extra body parts, for these questioners covet thy refrigerator that overfloweth with organs. But thou know better than to question those who would arrive at thy house in the middle of the night carrying plastic bags with people parts. Instead, keep thy mouth shut and reflect upon thy body of work and all the people thou hast helped. Realize that, if it were not for all the money, their health would be thy greatest reward.

Stealing the small bag of peanuts from the woman sleeping next to thee on the airplane

---

They shall not be ashamed in the evil time: and in the days of famine they shall be satisfied.

(Psalms 37:19)

---

ittle choice didst thou have when the stewardesses would not respond to thy seventh call-button push. Knoweth this: If the woman sitting next to thee were hungry, she'd be awake and eating those peanuts. Thou art just filling a basic human need and if thou can do it without waking thy seatmate, so much the better. And who is to know? Maybe this woman is deathly allergic to peanuts and thou art taking a legume bullet for her. Comfort thyself with this blanket of possible heroism, and if thou art still hungry, perhaps she hath some gum or mints in her purse.

Leaving thy mark on society with a permanent marker and a spray can

---

And thou shalt write them upon the posts of thy house, and on thy gates.

(Deuteronomy 6:9)

According to the Good Book, the fact that thou dost not own property should not stop thee from writing thy name, a clever pseudonym, or simple obscenities on the property of others. Practice thy craft upon stop signs, walls, and slow-moving farm animals. Treasure thy contributions to the landscape, for thy crude scribbling is in equal parts artistic and devaluing.

Informing a friend who said that thou wert capricious and irrational that she is forever dead to thee

---

For now I will stretch out my hand, that I may smite thee and thy people with pestilence; and thou shalt be cut off from the earth.

(Exodus 9:15)

The betrayal by a friend is always harsh. Just ask Jesus. If a friend hath turned against thee in some manner—let's say they have claimed thou art unreasonable—thou must act immediately to let this person know that their actions are hurtful and therefore thou hast decided to nullify their existence. Call mutual friends and tell them to delete the accused from their minds, their address books, and the emergency phone tree. The person who maligned thee needeth to be publicly scorned, so feel free to put up posters of the slanderer around town with the word WHORE emblazoned upon their forehead in red marker.

Being discovered on thy neighbors' roof carrying their silver tea service

*Speak now in the ears of the people,
and let every man borrow of his neighbour,
and every woman of her neighbour, jewels
of silver, and jewels of gold.*

(Exodus 11:2)

The Bible teacheth that charity starts at home—it's just that thou hast decided to begin at someone else's home. Thy neighbors' home is always good for charitable donations because of its proximity, and they might have already given thee a key. No matter if thou art unlocking the back door or casting a brick through their picture window, remember to wear a ski mask, as it gets quite chilly at night. Make certain, when thou art rifling through thy neighbors' prized possessions, to concentrate on taking any jewelry as it can be melted down and sold. Avoid stealing the television, as visiting neighbors might question their charitable contribution to thy rumpus room.

Creating a scene at the parent-teacher conference

I will meet them as a bear that is bereaved of her whelps, and will rend the caul of their heart, and there will I devour them like a lion: the wild beast shall tear them.

(Hosea 13:8)

How dare public education not meet the individual needs of thy children? If the evidence of thy copulation did not get into advanced-placement math class or the shiv they made in wood shop hath resulted in a week long suspension, make sure that those who stand against thee pay for their temerity. Let parents with a sense of decorum stand off to the side as thou drop to the floor and melt down like a nuclear plant without sufficient cooling water. Wail, beg, slap the floor with thine hands, cry out for help and then push away anyone who offers it. Knock down chairs, sob, anything to make thyself the unwelcome center of attention. Eventually, just to get thee to leave, thy demands will be met and thou will have arrived at the Promised Land of thy desires.

Taking measures to ensure that thou shalt never be asked to participate in a bake sale again

---

And thou shalt eat it as barley cakes, and thou shalt bake it with dung that cometh out of man, in their sight.

(Ezekiel 4:12)

Dig deep within thee if thou hast chosen to take the "nuclear option" in regard to a bake sale. The slothful will purchase store-bought baked goods and put them on a plate, but those who feel their cause is a righteous one shall go way beyond that, to a point where thou shalt never be asked to participate in anything ever again and will forever be shunned by the community. Obviously, this is a small price to pay for freedom.

Burning thy plastic recycling within view of thy self-righteous environmentalist neighbors

Who hath given him a charge over the earth? or who hath disposed the whole world?

(Job 34:13)

If ye art both going to be long dead before the ice caps melt away, what art thy neighbors so worried about? Truly, thy neighbors with their rotting compost pile and goat lawn mower have gone too far in their quest to save the Earth. The Lord knows that there is nobody holier than thee, so put these pretenders in their place by balancing their efforts with thine own. If they religiously recycle their cardboard, burn thine in the backyard. If they stop using their car to preserve fossil fuels, then burn fossils. Basically, thy responses will always involve burning.

Using charitable donations to thy church to decorate thine home like a casino

He overlaid also the house, the beams, the posts, and the walls thereof, and the doors thereof, with gold; and graved cherubims on the walls.

(2 Chronicles 3:7)

It should not be a surprise that the Lord, much like crows, enjoys sparkly things. His appreciation of items that sparkle or shimmer has been passed on to thee; after all, we are made in His image. Therefore it would be sinful not to gild thy stately sanctuary with all manner of silver, platinum, and gold all shined to a reflective state. Blessed be thou also for thy liberal use of cherubs throughout the house. If there is one thing God loves, besides all of mankind, it is fat, winged babies.

Lying to vegetarians about what was in the lasagna thou madest

But he said unto them, I have
meat to eat that ye know not of.
(John 4:32)

Openly deride not the eschewers of meat, for certainly their mental illness must have been caused by being dropped as babies or in rodeo accidents. Pity them for their inability to partake of the euphoric world of meat. However, this compassion must end at thy front door, especially if non-meat-eating visitors are expecting more than coleslaw for dinner. Perhaps a lack of protein causeth them not to realize the absolute impossibility of creating an entrée without meat. As thou would an Easter egg, solve these problems by hiding the meat from them. If discovered, claim a miracle.

---

*They shall call the people unto the mountain;
there they shall offer sacrifices of righteousness: for they shall suck of the abundance of
the seas, and of treasures hid in the sand.*

(Deuteronomy 33:19)

Art thou one who watcheth pirate movies and believeth piracy is a victimless crime, that stabbing and keelhauling are great fun? According to the Bible, thou art absolutely correct. Blessed be thou if thou hast decided that thy life is at sea harassing the hapless, because thou will be a member of the last group that can pull off large hoop earrings, shoulder parrots, and eye patches. Additionally, thou will be doing a community service, for pirates are the only natural predators of cruise ships and oil rigs. Without thee, the sea is awash with boundless capitalism, so the Almighty encourageth thee to put thy peg leg down and take a stand, as well as anything else that isn't nailed down.

Waking up drunk two miles from home and wearing only one shoe

---

The gin shall take him by the heel, and the robber shall prevail against him.

(Job 18:9)

Dread not if thou awakest miles from home with sexual organs drawn on thy face with permanent marker and thy wallet long gone. Alcohol is a magical liquid that in one moment can encourage fellowship among men and the next can be a flying carpet to a far-off location, usually an alley, a ditch, or a stranger's bedroom. The Bible instructs thee not to lament the loss of a single shoe; instead, celebrate the retention of its remaining brother and thy pants. If thou art to blame alcohol for thy problems, do it later when thou assign it accountability for all of thine accumulated problems and repeated court dates.

Shacking up with an older gentleman with skin like a wallet, beachfront property, and enough money to keep thee happy

He lodgeth with one Simon a tanner, whose house is by the sea side: he shall tell thee what thou oughtest to do.

(Acts 10:6)

There is no shame in sharing a home with a man who pays thy bills and is two years older than thy father. No, thou shalt embrace that special connection that thou seem to have with middle-aged men who own red, convertible sports cars and squeeze themselves into jeans made for twenty-year-olds. Jealous naysayers might claim that benefactors such as these are just trying to recapture their youth, but naught be wrong with thee assisting in their quest for longevity, especially if they have promised to buy thee a new wardrobe and let thee drive their boat around.

Taking a penny but never actually giving a penny to the little dish at the convenience store

---

Shew me the tribute money.
And they brought unto him a penny.

(Matthew 22:19)

Nowhere dost it say that thou must leave a penny if thou art to take one. Indeed, this is lunacy, for where art the profit in that? Thou art under no legal obligation to give a penny. There is a choice, and thou hast chosen to take a penny. Embrace then the Godliness of thy decision to partake of the penny dish, and leave others to their demented contributions.

Buying an SUV so large that thou needest stairs to get to the driver's seat

---

And they worshipped the dragon which gave power unto the beast: and they worshipped the beast, saying, Who is like unto the beast? who is able to make war with him?

(Revelation 13:4)

Closer art thee to thy God when thou art sitting in the driver's seat of thy SUV. The people in the cars around thee look like little ants from thy perch, and there is no reason that thou should not feel rightfully superior to members of the insect world. It matters not that thy vehicle gets .5 mile per gallon—if thou does not make use of natural resources, someone else will. As an added safety measure, thou canst drive over the subcompacts in front of thee, crushing them below thy righteous wheels. If required, thou could probably off-road to Heaven.

Embezzling from the company's pension fund in order to buy thyself a yacht

Men do not despise a thief, if he steal to satisfy his soul when he is hungry.

(Proverbs 6:30)

There are different kinds of hunger. For one it might be the hunger of an empty stomach, for another it might be a hunger for an ascot and a captain's hat. Be assured: if those who would have benefited from the pension fund knew how much thou desired the yacht, they would not howl for thine imprisonment. Instead they would applaud thine one-mindedness in the pursuit of thy goal. Perhaps if thou offer them a ride on thy boat, it shall balm their emotional wounds. If that still does not work, let them wear the hat.

Alternately shaking and nodding thy head vigorously at a meeting when thou hast no idea what is actually being discussed

But let your communication be, Yea, yea; Nay, nay: for whatsoever is more than these cometh of evil.

(Matthew 5:37)

Thine employer feels that thine opinion is important only because it matches his own exactly. In fact, thou hast not had an original idea since thou were hired, and the Bible tells thee that this is acceptable, even preferable. Thine indiscriminate devotion to thy boss, along with thine ignorance of all subjects, will help thee move up in the company. An important caveat is that thou must remember never to expound on thy agreements—just nod or shake thine head to match the emotional state of thy boss, and then ask to use the bathroom.

Keeping thy fabulous alter ego and size fourteen pumps hidden from thy son

---

A man shall not take his father's wife, nor discover his father's skirt.

(Deuteronomy 22:30)

What thou hast locked in thy closet is nobody's business but thine and thy adoring fans at the cabaret. Thy son, though he shares his father's fine tenor voice, does not need to know what thou dost in the privacy of thy dressing room. Thou hast the right to privacy and to roses from admirers. However, keep an eye out for some ruby slippers in his size, for thou hast a great Ethel Merman–Judy Garland duet in mind that would be a complete showstopper.

Sending thine ill-begotten currency to a foreign country to be laundered

Not greedy of filthy lucre.

(1 Timothy 3:3)

Whether thou earn thy gold dealing in large swathes of Florida swamp country or simply selling foreign brides through the Internet, there will always be those, such as the Internal Revenue Service and the Treasury Department, who choose to believe that thy money is somehow unclean. At these times, it is best to remember what the Bible teaches—cleanliness is next to Godliness—so do not hold on to this "dirty" currency. If the Lord wanted thee in a minimum-security prison and for the United States government to have thy money, he would not have created Switzerland, where moneychangers are happy to handle all of thy laundering needs.

Refusing to listen to those who would tell thee to stop running with scissors

But they refused to hearken, and pulled away the shoulder, and stopped their ears, that they should not hear.

(Zechariah 7:11)

thers, in life, will attempt to give thee their counsel and the "gift" of their experience. It is essential that thou ignore all of this "help," for it will only poison thine ability to make thine own choices. Instead, jam thy fingers into thine ears and chant "la-la-la-la" as others attempt to share their knowledge with thee. Embrace the chance to make the exact same mistakes of those who went before thee, whether it be sticking a fork into an electrical outlet or making idle threats to large people. They say that those who do not understand history will be doomed to repeat it, but there is no reason that thou should pay heed to that.

Stuffing ballot boxes to steal the election for thy presidential candidate

---

And in very deed for this cause have I raised thee up, for to shew in thee my power; and that my name may be declared throughout all the earth.

(Exodus 9:16)

In thine heart thou knowest that something as important as an election should not be left to the whim of the general populace. No, the public has a history of poor decision making, especially when it comes to national elections. Remember, thou art only thinking of the good of the people when thou and 125,000 deceased voters make the decision for them. If thou art successful, thy name will be remembered forever. Perhaps chanted by angry people with torches, but remembered nonetheless. Thy candidate will certainly reward thee with an ambassadorship to a tropical nation, and perhaps, depending on how far thou hast gone to ensure the election for them, a presidential pardon may be in the offing.

Blaming the owner of a parked car for a minor auto accident that tore off his bumper

---

Behold, I go forward, but he is not there; and backward, but I cannot perceive him.

(Job 23:8)

If thou hast bent another's fender or ripped it cleanly off their car, gird thyself for the queries of the jackals known as "insurance adjusters." The Bible teaches that thou shouldst protest thine innocence loudly, and if they do not believeth thee, protest it more. Anyway, what business is it of theirs that thy vehicle might have some pre-existing problems caused by driving into a garbage truck? Throughout this process, remember that part of defensive driving is refusing to admit to anything.

Eating someone else's lunch out of the communal refrigerator at work

*Stolen waters are sweet, and
bread eaten in secret is pleasant.*

(Proverbs 9:17)

Just as food tastes better at a restaurant, so too does the lunch of another. There is something about forbidden but readily available delights that makes a meal that much sweeter. Worry not for the person whose sandwich and tiny bag of carrots thou hast purloined, for their hunger can be sated with selections from the vending machine. Be certain to deny forcefully that thou art the culprit, for this will make thy stolen treat even more flavorful. If questions persist, suggest that the janitorial staff have looked quite guilty.

Yelling at the police when they ask thee to turn down Led Zeppelin in the early hours of the morning

---

He teareth himself in his anger:
shall the earth be forsaken for thee? and
shall the rock be removed out of his place?

(Job 18:4)

---

ake heed! There is no greater sign of God's eternal love for man than 70s rock bands such as Led Zeppelin, the Who, and the Starland Vocal Band. Led Zeppelin's *Houses of the Holy* is clearly God's type of music, because it has "holy" in the title and it is loud enough for Him to hear from His Heavenly Throne. So, if at three o'clock in the morning thy neighbors ask thee to turn the music down, they might as well be telling thee to turn the God down. Who wins then? The Devil, and perhaps the neighbors' eardrums. Instead, turn up the music, and when the police knock on the door, crank it up louder because someone within a mile of thine home is always in need of some extra God-loving.

Starting a lice epidemic
in thy community

———— ◇◇◇ ————

*And the magicians did so with their enchant-
ments to bring forth lice, but they could not:
so there were lice upon man, and upon beast.*

(Exodus 8:18)

———— ◇◇◇ ————

Feeleth no shame for the thriftiness that causes occasional, communitywide health issues. Just because a hat thou found in the gutter and chose to wear was full of hair-borne parasites that hath spread to the general public, it does not mean that thou hast done wrong. Furthermore, take pride that thou hast put money away, perhaps saving it for something important like a television, a very large television. As for the people around thee who have resorted to medicated shampoos and those special lice combs, absolve thyself of any wrongdoing, for it is always best to lay fault for such epidemics at the feet of the imaginary, such as magicians or werewolves.

Blindsiding a woman with a clothes rack because she was heading toward the store's last pair of strappy sandals

For the fashion of this world passeth away.

(1 Corinthians 7:31)

If our savior, Jesus Christ, would not be caught dead in sandals with socks, why wouldst thou? The world of style is constantly changing and thou must do all in thy power to keep up with it, even if it means endangering the safety of others as thou careen dangerously through boutiques looking for the next "it" accessory. Let thyself strayest not from the prize, for today's paragon of couture could be tomorrow's fashion victim, especially if thou art predicting the triumphant return of the hair shirt and rope belts.

Selling thy country's secret missile plans to a foreign government

And the spies saw a man come forth out of the city, and they said unto him, Shew us, we pray thee, the entrance into the city, and we will shew thee mercy.

(Judges 1:24)

Thou shalt not speak ill of the United States, for it hath assured its people the rights of life, liberty, and the opportunity to sell treasonous secrets at high prices to attractive spies from foreign governments. No matter whether thou agree with another country's politics or lack of human rights, thou must appreciate how much they're willing to pay thee for the plans for nuclear missiles, submarines, and the like. Art thou betraying thy country? Yes, this should be obvious. But fearest not, for the Almighty hath blessed thy nation above all others with the destructive imagination to come up with new weaponry that will be much more destructive and terrifying than the goods thou sold.

Pretending to go to work each day but instead hanging out at the local tavern buying lottery tickets

---

What profit hath he that worketh in that wherein he laboureth?

(Ecclesiastes 3:9)

Where is the pleasure in labor? Why wouldeth one work when there is an overflowing pot of gold awaiting those who would select the correctly numbered Ping-Pong balls? Put away the sweat of thy brow and put forward one dollar. Then sit back, have a beer, and imagine the sweet consequences of winning. Perhaps make a list of thine enemies who will pay the most when thou claimest thy sure windfall. If thou dost not win on thy first try, dismay not, for victory is surely just around the corner. Have another drink and visualize the small island thou can buy and imprison thine enemies on.

Being the scourge of local all-thy-can-eat buffets

Man shall not live by bread alone.

(Matthew 4:4)

The Lord giveth many blessings unto man, not the least of which are top-thine-own-sundae bars and all-thy-can-eat buffets. And if it is God's will that thou art truly to eat all thy medically can, thou must avoid the traps that buffet owners throw into thy path, such as bread. As Jesus cast the moneylenders from the temple, so shalt thou topple the baskets of warm rolls, for these are the work of the Devil. Then knock away those who would block thee from such items as shrimp, fried scallops, and roast beef, and overflow thyself with food, for to do so is to fill thyself with the spirit of the Almighty.

Marrying thy first cousin
at thy family compound

*And now it is true that I am thy
near kinsman: howbeit there is a
kinsman nearer than I.*

(Ruth 3:12)

The Bible brimmeth with important information, such as the fact that there is nothing wrong with entering into wedlock with someone whose chromosomal makeup is almost identical to thine own. Thou and thy cousin have always been close. What, besides the violation of several Federal laws, would be wrong with getting a little closer? The advantages to such a union are manyfold, as thou hast already met thine in-laws and thy partner is a probable kidney match. Lastly, if thou art lucky, thou won't have to change last names.

Secretly moving away while thy child is at college

And he said, I will hide my face from them, I will see what their end shall be: for they are a very froward generation, children in whom is no faith.

(Deuteronomy 32:20)

The Bible knows that not every parent suffers from an empty nest. Quite the contrary, some sensible parents have awaited the dates of their children's emancipation as eagerly as they waited for the legal use of alcohol on their own twenty-first birthdays. If thou count thyself amongst this group, there is no reason thou cannot set thyself free as thou send thy children into the world. As doth the mother bird, push them out of the nest, put the wind beneath their wings, and then, just in case they decide to fly back, move the nest and change thy phone number. When they eventually find thee, they might even thank thee.

Displaying a growing affection for thy rich relatives

---

*Nevertheless they did flatter
him with their mouth, and they lied
unto him with their tongues.*

(Psalms 78:36)

Truly there be much one can learn from the older members of thy family, especially what they plan to do with their money after they are metaphysically catapulted off of this mortal coil. Show thy respect for thy sickliest—and wealthiest—elders by sitting at their knees, listening enraptured to their stories, and assuring them that they hath always been thy favorite relation. Compliment their many fine qualities and take their side on any long-term family feud, no matter how petty or destructive it may be to family togetherness. As for thine elderly relatives without money, a postcard is acceptable.

Paying a dollar's worth of hush money to a child after climbing out of their parents' window wearing only a bedspread

———————◇◇◇———————

Charity shall cover the multitude of sins.
(1 Peter 4:8)

———————◇◇◇———————

Embrace charity in all its many forms, be it donating a wing to a hospital, not laughing at a person who falls down an escalator, or paying a child for their silence. There art those who say that giving is the true reward, and they art correct, especially when thee wilt get something in return. The Bible tells thee that any performed deed of generosity wipes thy ledger clean of sin. Therefore it is in thy best interests to give when thou can, or at least when thou art planning any major transgressions against humanity.

Cheerfully giving out dental health pamphlets and floss to disappointed trick-or-treaters

---

They have corrupted themselves, their spot is not the spot of his children: they are a perverse and crooked generation.

(Deuteronomy 32:5)

The future lieth with children and, verily, that is terrifying. It is up to thee to chart a path for youth, no matter if they are thy children or not. Take any opportunity to enlighten the younger set on how to better themselves, whether that be by lecturing on dental health at Halloween or on the fact that they should not stare at the sun. They shall probably not thank thee for thy good works, in fact they shall probably pelt thine home with garbage—but thou should find much comfort in thy righteousness.

Downloading every song ever written from the Internet for free

───────────⧓───────────

And he spake three thousand proverbs: and his songs were a thousand and five.

(1 Kings 4:32)

───────────⧓───────────

The Internet is a wondrous invention, heavy with offers to increase the size of one's manhood, videos of celebrities copulating, and free music. Minions of Satan, also known as "the music industry," want thee to pay for the complimentary music that thou hast plucked from the digital ether, but pay them no heed. Instead, fall to thy knees and praise a miracle that is as wondrous as that of the loaves and the fishes, as one purchased CD has turned into 15,000 free downloads.

Partaking in the epic battle that is thy family's Thanksgiving dinner

―――――――――――――∞―――――――――――――

Though ye offer me burnt offerings and your meat offerings, I will not accept them: neither will I regard the peace offerings of your fat beasts.

(Amos 5:22)

―――――――――――――∞―――――――――――――

The Bible reminds us that families are a constant source of blessings, though when a request to pass the potatoes turns into a threat of a knife fight, these blessings may seem rather meager. Soften not thine outlook just because others feel that family reconciliation is a worthy goal during the holidays. No, hold on to thine undercurrent of rage and nurture it like a campfire. Every implied insult or question about what thou art doing with thy life is another log on that fire, with presentations of photo albums and home movies being as gasoline thrown on for effect. What about the meals that thy family provides thee? A trick to reduce thy defenses, and one to which thou must not surrender.

Drunkenly practicing karate
at a friend's party

*And I took the two tables, and
cast them out of my two hands,
and brake them before your eyes.*

(Deuteronomy 9:17)

hine arms and legs are lethal weapons, especially
to imaginary ninjas and inanimate objects. What
better time to display thy self-taught prowess in
the martial arts than at a crowded social gathering? After
partaking of some alcoholic beverages, put thy gifts on
display by cartwheeling down the stairs or breaking a lamp
with a flying kick. Encourage others to throw empty beer
cans at thine head so that thou mightst attempt to chop
them out of the air. For the pièce de résistance, seek out a
friend who will break a piece of timber across thy forehead,
thus demonstrating thy mastery of self-defense.

Ending thy gluttonous slob of a roommate's residency by putting his couch and clothes on the lawn in the rain

―――――∞―――――

And he that eateth of the carcase of it shall wash his clothes, and be unclean until the even: he also that beareth the carcase of it shall wash his clothes, and be unclean until the even.

(Leviticus 11:40)

―――――∞―――――

Hath a roommate tarried too long in a house where he and his accumulated garbage are no longer welcome? Hast thy roommate consumed thy last frozen chicken burrito one time too many? Wouldst thou have burned his couch if it hadn't been made in the 1970s with plaid, flame-retardant materials? The Bible teaches that the legal rights of others should never stand in the way of thine happiness. If police arrive to question thine eviction, remind them that just as cleanliness is next to Godliness, so too are filth and gluttony a sure sign of Devil worship.

Bringing shame upon thy family by passing out in thy sister's wedding cake

And they shall say unto the elders of his city, This our son is stubborn and rebellious, he will not obey our voice; he is a glutton, and a drunkard.

(Deuteronomy 21:20)

I f thy parents have picked favorites amongst their children and thou were not even on the ballot, then thou should embrace thy least-favored position within thy family. Climb out on the extended limb of the family tree by not purchasing Christmas gifts and loudly complaining about thy banishment to the kids' table. Knowest that thy family members will only shake their heads sadly in response to anything thou dost as the black sheep, so if thou preferest to dress in a gorilla suit for a family photo or drive the station wagon into the pool, feelest free.

Enhancing thy pleasure
with a bit of pain

Thy rod and thy staff they comfort me.

(Psalms 23:4)

Sometimes when thou hast known someone "in the Biblical sense" and there hath been much rending of garments and transgressing each other in various positions and public places, the shine comes off the shekel a bit. There is nothing wrong with spicing up the relationship, adding some myrrh to the frankincense, so to speak. Tell thy beloved that thou hast sinned, and suggest that they beateth this wickedness out of thee with a whip and riding crop. If necessary, remind them that thy nipples are also full of sin. Or play out roles such as Sodom versus Gomorrah or the angry chariot driver and the unbridled ass.

Surprising thy parents
by moving back home

Honour thy father and thy mother:
that thy days may be long upon the land
which the Lord thy God giveth thee.
(Exodus 20:12)

---

ittle did thou realize the high cost of housing when thou first moved out of thy parents' home. Luckily for thee, they had not changed the locks when thou returned later that day. Do not let the fact that thy twin bed is covered with *Star Wars* sheets dissuade thee from moving home. In fact, if thou stays long enough, God, who is the land Lord for all, hath promised one day that the house shall belong to thee. And then thou can stay up as late as thou wants to watch television. Until that time consider thy parents to be rather uptight roommates who just happen to have baby pictures of thee.

Downloading pornography that is a little beyond the bounds of good taste

─────────◦◦◦─────────

For she doted upon their paramours, whose flesh is as the flesh of asses, and whose issue is like the issue of horses.

(Ezekiel 23:20)

─────────◦◦◦─────────

The Bible commands that thou shouldst feel no shame in seeking carnal stimulation that is beyond the pale. Just as there are more ice cream flavors than chocolate and vanilla, so too do people such as thou hath different sexual proclivities. Why should it matter that thy carnal interests are the equivalent of mango ice cream with oysters—satisfying to thee but abhorrent to others? Lick deeply of thy personal flavor and allow thyself to seek out titillation wherever thou can find it, whether it be the Internet or department store underwear circulars.

Refusing to yield the microphone at karaoke

Neglect not the gift that is in thee.

(1 Timothy 4:14)

reat talent lieth within thee—it might just take a bit of digging to expose it. Do not let this stop thee from performing, however. Perhaps uncovering thy talent is just a matter of repetition or volume, so feel free to embrace both methods when in public. Ignore protestations from the less talented who may claim that thou art harming their ears, for they are witnessing the birth of thy gift. Remember, it would be sinful not to reach for the stars, although if they are still out of thy grasp, thou might want to try singing with more vibrato.

Letting the world know about thy friend's third nipple

That which ye have spoken in the ear in closets shall be proclaimed upon the house tops.

(Luke 12:3)

Verily, thy friend should have known better than to have told thee about their aberration. They should realize that the only joy one finds in secrets is in divulging them to people who will be visibly aghast at the information. The Bible vindicates thee for not being able to keep a confidence for more than five minutes, as that behavior is to be expected, especially from thee. And, truly, if people want not their medical oddities to be discussed in a public forum, then they shouldn't tell anyone about them or, for that matter, see a doctor.

Starting thine own charitable foundation that deposits funds directly into thy checking account

---

And all they that were about them strengthened their hands with vessels of silver, with gold, with goods, and with beasts, and with precious things, beside all that was willingly offered.

(Ezra 1:6)

S weet charity—how it soothes the soul. If thou art in need, no matter what thy definition of need actually is, allow thyself to start a charity to benefit the person who is closest to thy heart: thee. Recruit potential donors by impressing them with thy charitable deeds, making sure thou never mentionest high-definition television or trips to Aruba as needs of thy charity. Perhaps donors would appreciate a thank-thee note—just make certain thou writest in crayon, claiming to be a disadvantaged seven-year-old child from a country of which they have never heard.

Claiming that the accident
that dented thy car's side
mirror was also responsible
for thy severe whiplash

---

*And if any mischief follow, then thou shalt
give life for life, eye for eye, tooth for tooth,
hand for hand, foot for foot, burning for
burning, wound for wound, stripe for stripe.*

(Exodus 21:23–21:25)

As we all know, insurance adjusters art in the employ of the Devil and will all eventually burn in eternal fire. But what can thou do until that time? For starters, there is nothing wrong with carrying a spare neck brace in thy glove compartment for the occasional fender bender. One of the many blessings the Lord hath given to humanity is compensatory damages in civil cases and if, Biblically speaking, an eye equals an eye, isn't the psychological trauma over thy scratched bumper worth a few thousand dollars? Just because you can't point to the pain doesn't mean you won't eventually feel it.

Improving foreign relations and thy personal supply of pharmaceuticals by sneaking across the border at three o'clock in the morning

---

For by thee I have run through a troop:
by my God have I leaped over a wall.

(2 Samuel 22:30)

Do boundary shouldeth exist between the brothers and sisters of the Lord's creation, no matter what the Border Patrol hath said. For this reason, thine ability to hide behind large objects and trees is truly a passport to adventure and if thou time thy run correctly, thou shouldst have little trouble getting into other countries. Once in foreign locales, thou canst partake in the local practices and perhaps return to thy country with samplings of exotic goods and "medications" that are not available in pharmacies, which thou can then resell at a massive profit.

Stubbornly insisting that
the United States is bordered
by the countries of Canada,
Mexico, and New Mexico

---

*For in much wisdom is much grief: and he
that increaseth knowledge increaseth sorrow.*

(Ecclesiastes 1:18)

---

oth thine head feel hot when thou art required to do prolonged thinking? Then rejoice! The Lord loves thee better that way. The Bible teaches that knowledge is painful, so consider it a blessing from above every time thou staple thy thumb or are stuck in a revolving door. To continue along thy path of ignorance, avoid such items as daily newspapers, road maps, and medication instructions. Things that are okay: Websites with more than three flashing banners ads, lead paint, and movies with previews that show multiple groin injuries.

Talking incessantly about thy six-pack abs and powerful eighteen-inch pecs

---

But he spake of the temple of his body.
(John 2:21)

Thou hast labored greatly to improve thyself physically; if others do not recognize the flesh sculpture that is thy body, then thou shalt remind them. Accentuate thy physical positives by wearing T-shirts that are two sizes too small and through the unrestrained use of spandex. Speak loudly of what thou canst bench and, if necessary, kick sand in the faces of the meek, for their weakness shall accentuate thy strength. If necessary, point to thine arm muscles and ask, "Is there a vet around here? Because these pythons are sick."

Treating thine ailments with a blend of cough syrup, household cleaning products, and a bottle of gin

---

Physician, heal thyself.

(Luke 4:23)

With the advances of modern medicine, there is little need to consult a doctor. Pharmacies offer a wide array of over-the-counter medication, and the Bible says that if mixed correctly, they can put thee under the table and well on the way to recovery, no matter what ailment hath bothered thee. In fact, half the joy of self-medication is the journey of discovery, determining what blends cure thee of all symptoms and which will require a return trip to the emergency room. As for the warning labels printed on the sides of medication bottles, these are just a starting point, a strong suggestion, if thou will. And why stop at curing thy cold when thou can go much further by creating hallucinogenic cough drops or methamphetamines?

Observing thy neighbors with high-powered binoculars and night-vision goggles

---

Therefore let us not sleep, as do others;
but let us watch and be sober.

(1 Thessalonians 5:6)

Many praises on thee for keeping watch over thy flock at night. Do thy neighbors know that they are part of thy flock? It matters not. Thy lonely vigil must go without reward and thine heroism must go unrecognized. If not for thee, who would keep a watchful eye on thy neighbor with a heart condition whilst he puts on his wife's makeup? Who would be there to videotape thy single neighbor who prefers to vacuum naked? Nobody, that's who.

Convincing an army general in a small, remote country that his best option is a coup

---

And thou shalt speak unto him, and put words in his mouth: and I will be with thy mouth, and with his mouth, and will teach you what ye shall do.

(Exodus 4:15)

Blessed art thou for thy desire to do charitable work in countries with untapped oil reserves. It is obvious that El Generalissimo wants much for his country and, with the exceptions of the lashings, he is good to his people. If God guides thee thusly, convince the general that for the continued well-being of his country, it is necessary that he seize control of the local radio station, surround the international airport with tanks, and send the democratically elected government into forced exile. Let him know that thou hath no self-interest in his actions, although God has told thee not to say no to drilling rights in the northern part of the country.

Getting ready for the big game with a syringe of human growth hormone jammed into thy buttock

---

He that dasheth in pieces is come up before thy face: keep the munition, watch the way, make thy loins strong, fortify thy power mightily.

(Nahum 2:1)

---

ictory is thine, sayeth the Lord, as long as thou art willing to inject intravenously substances derived from the thyroid glands of chimpanzees. Too often competitions are won by those who are the fastest or the strongest. Luckily for thee, modern science has managed to level the playing field with chemicals that are just as God-given as talent. Feel no shame in the excess hair that hath grown between thy brows or thy constant boiling rage, for thou art a winner and nobody can take that away from thee. Unless, of course, they decide to take a urine sample.

Gawking openly in the locker room when the man next to thee drops his towel

---

For they cast down every man his rod, and they became serpents: but Aaron's rod swallowed up their rods.

(Exodus 7:12)

There is nothing wrong with taking a gander at the men who mill about thee in the gym, particularly when their towels are askew. The human body is the Lord's creation, and by staring at another man's assets it is as if thou art staring directly into the crotch of God. It is only right that the nakedness of other men should be celebrated and/or ogled. Allow thyself to be free from the shame of staring too long, and allow thyself to indulge in the magical parade of nakedness that surrounds thee. Just make certain that thou ask before thou dost any touching.

Sleeping with every single man in thy zip code

And the river shall bring forth frogs abundantly, which shall go up and come into thine house, and into thy bedchamber, and upon thy bed, and into the house of thy servants, and upon thy people, and into thine ovens, and into thy kneading troughs.

(Exodus 8:3)

The term "whore" is bandied about too much, especially when yelled in thy direction or keyed onto thy car. What, thou must ask those who would belittle thee, is wrong with dating? In thy quest to find Mr. Right thou must go through many Mr. Wrongs, and why should they not buy thee dinner? And if thou decidest to recompense their kindness with some physical affection, that should be nobody's business but thine and the male half of the town. They did buy thee dinner after all, or a Popsicle at the least.

Threatening the life of thy friend, the morning person

He that blesseth his friend with a loud voice, rising early in the morning, it shall be counted a curse to him.

(Proverbs 27:14)

Is there no person or falling object that can silence the braying of thy friend in the morning? Doth he not realize that his voice is the bowling ball and thy consciousness a fragile set of tiny glass animals? That his very voice makes thine ears desire to bleed? Silence the miscreant who would try to awaken thee from thy reverie with threats and invectives. Maybe the best way for thee to wake is to pour thyself a hot cup of black coffee and throw it at the head of thy deafening problem.

Pulling the fire alarm
in an attempt to get out of
work ten minutes early

*As yet exaltest thou thyself against my
people, that thou wilt not let them go?*

(Exodus 9:17)

Art thou besieged by thy employer's demands and the heaviness of thy inbox? Art thou certain that the little hand on the clock just ticked back one minute? Dismay not. Throw off the heavy chains of thy employment, break the alarm box glass, and head toward the exit light. Hast thou been warned about falsely using the fire alarm? Then set a small fire in the kitchenette. If this doth not work, simply find an alternate route of egress, perhaps crawling through the ductwork or jumping from the roof onto a passing truck. Know this: whatever the cost of thine escape, it is worth it.

Burying evidence in thy neighbor's yard and then phoning in an anonymous tip to the police department

---

For wheresoever the carcase is, there will the eagles be gathered together.
(Matthew 24:28)

None are free from sin and, sadly, thou art less free than others. Even more regrettable is that the local authorities have begun to realize thy level of sin. Certainly the time has come to unearth thy basement, relocate the evidence of thy previous misdoings to thy neighbors' backyard, and place a call to the police, using a foreign accent. Thy neighbors might go to prison, but that is acceptable, for they know they are innocent. Why should thou pay for thy crimes? Thou knowest thou art a sinner, and that is enough for the Lord.

Missing thy grandmother's 100th birthday to go to Las Vegas

Absent in body, but present in spirit
(1 Corinthians 5:3)

Dost thou have conflicting engagements? Does one—let's say a bachelorette party in Las Vegas—sound more desirable than another—perhaps celebrating a century of thy grandmother's existence? Thou should feel no remorse if thou choose to inhale tequila shots in the desert rather than tapioca at thy grandmother's retirement community—for, through a miracle of the Bible, thou may send thy body in one direction whilst thy spirit goes in another. Take heed, however, this miracle of physical truancy is not accepted for jury duty or prison sentences.

Using pity and hysterical sobbing in an attempt to get thy date to stay the night

———◇◇◇———

Now therefore, I pray you, tarry ye also here this night, that I may know what the Lord will say unto me more.

(Numbers 22:19)

———◇◇◇———

When it comes to needs of the heart and matters carnal, there is little wrong with begging and groveling. If the one thou desirest to lie with rejects thee, be mindful that there is no low too great or debasement too awkward to put thyself through. Do not arrest thyself from speaking in a voice two octaves higher than thy normal speaking voice or holding thy breath until thy beloved acquiesces. Tell the desired one that it is the Almighty's will that ye become entwined, and if they wouldst lieth with thee, they might just see the light. If thou thinkest it would help, throw thyself onto the floor, grab onto thy beloved's leg, and let them drag thee around the floor until their heart softens or pity eventually prevails.

Tearing around the neighborhood in thy car making chicken noises at anyone who refuses to race thee

The chariots shall rage in the streets, they shall justle one against another in the broad ways: they shall seem like torches, they shall run like the lightnings.

(Nahum 2:4)

he Almighty has blessed thee with a lead foot and the temerity to pass on the double line, so why should thou not employ thy gift of speed? Certainly other drivers must realize that thy crash helmet is no joke. Allow thyself to burn rubber through the streets, hog the road, and unbottle the lightning of thy subcompact's engine. Ignore those who would laugh at thee, for soon they shall be but dots in thy rearview mirror. Perhaps if thou were to paint flames on the side of thy vehicle, they would take thee more seriously.

Selling nude photos of thine ex-boyfriend to a website called www.regrettablenakedness.com

---

Thy nakedness shall be uncovered, yea, thy shame shall be seen: I will take vengeance, and I will not meet thee as a man.

(Isaiah 47:3)

Hast thou been rejected by a former lover? What art thou supposed to do with the objects that remind thee of him, such as digital images of his nakedness and various engorgements? The pagans would tell thee that burning the photos would help release the pain from thine heart, but then this kind of poor decision making is why all pagans roam lost in the woods. Instead of taking advice from those who bay at the moon, balm thine heart by making a profit through thy former beloved's pain. Sell his photos to a website, laying bare the faults of he who hath rejected thee, and leaving him burning on the stake of public humiliation.

Allowing an oil tanker driven by a drunken captain passage through a marine sanctuary

And I will give it into the hands of the strangers for a prey, and to the wicked of the earth for a spoil; and they shall pollute it.

(Ezekiel 7:21)

L ike weeds, nature just keeps on growing, no matter how much cutting and despoiling are done. Therefore worry not about thine actions which threaten endangered species, for they have a habit of popping up in zoos and stuffed in museum exhibits. Anyway, if these animals are so prized for their evolution, why can they not live in oil? It seemeth that without this adaptation they shall just end up as dead ducks.

Raising thy neighbor's cat from near death with a pair of jumper cables

---

In a moment, in the twinkling of an eye, at the last trump: for the trumpet shall sound, and the dead shall be raised incorruptible, and we shall be changed.

(1 Corinthians 15:52)

How wert thou to know that the next-door cat was sleeping underneath thy car when thou backed out? Now it is up to thee to take action for the comatose feline. Combine thy little knowledge of veterinary medicine with thy proficiency in automobile mechanics to bring the animal back for its ninth life. If thou art successful in the resuscitation and thy neighbors notice not the scorch marks, then the secret can be all thine.

Leaving threats made of words from cut-up newspapers on thy coworker's desk

And the Lord answered me, and said, Write the vision, and make it plain upon tables, that he may run that readeth it.

(Habakkuk 2:2)

Art thou having a civil disagreement at thine office over a name for the softball team or what kind of chips should be in the vending machine? Certainly a mutual exchange of ideas would be a way to solve thy problems, but, the Bible asks, where is the fun in that? Instead, use glue and scissors to create anonymous threatening missives that are clearly the work of a lunatic. Then sit back and watch as thine opponent turneth into a quivering wreck who eats lunch under his desk.

Yelling obscenities at the
people at the ski lodge who
laughed at thee when thou
passed them with one ski and
a mouthful of pine needles

---

*Speak, ye that ride on white asses, ye that
sit in judgment, and walk by the way.*

(Judges 5:10)

Rebuke those who would belittle thy sporting accomplishments, for they art seeking a way to highlight their own competency. Who art they to tell thee that the path of the righteous does not lead into the side of a ski-lift pylon? Thy continued failures are much more valuable than their knowledge, for thou hast learned the hard way not to point thyself directly down the mountain. Do not let them lord it over thee, for there is but one Lord above thee and if thou pray hard enough, He might make thine enemies ski into a chalet or a bear's den.

Repeatedly claiming thy Fifth Amendment rights against self-incrimination before a congressional hearing

Though wickedness be sweet in his mouth, though he hide it under his tongue.

(Job 20:12)

S peakest not if thine own words would imprison thee. It is best to sit in front of lawmakers, nod solemnly at their inquiries, then after a brief whisper from thine attorney, plead thy Fifth Amendment rights into the microphone. Repeat this again and again, until thou art excused from their presence. Know that God supports thine evasion of earthly justice, for He knows that thou would not do well in prison, especially with thy lack of upper-body strength and propensity to cry at night.

Writing bathroom wall accusations against the woman who refused to go on a date with thee

———— ✦ ————

For true and righteous are his judgments:
for he hath judged the great whore.
(Revelation 19:2)

———— ✦ ————

Disparaging another's character has its place in the Bible, especially if that person has hurt thy feelings in any manner. Thou art a catch, thy Mother has told thee on many occasions, and any woman who disagrees with that seems to be calling the woman who breastfed thee for six years a liar. And the only people who would malign thy Mother in that manner are whores and witches. Therefore, be not troubled by making groundless accusations against the woman who rejected thee, including the unsupportable fact that she is in a coven that eats children.

Telling thy boyfriend that thou art allergic to dogs when in fact thou just don't like the fur on thy clothes

---

Neither shalt thou lie with any beast to defile thyself therewith: neither shall any woman stand before a beast to lie down thereto: it is confusion.

(Leviticus 18:23)

Thou hast seen that look of disdain in a canine's beady eyes. That, the low growl, and raised hackles as thou try to shoo it off the couch. There is not room for the two of ye under one roof, and thou and the dog know it. Rejoice, for both the Good Book shares thy distaste for animals that would doggedly stand in the way. To this end, sneeze, gasp, and wheeze in the presence of the mangy beast. Snort pepper, if thou thinkst it will bring some poignancy to thy performance. Do not let these wolves in dogs' clothing dissuade thee from thy goal, which is them chained to a doghouse in the backyard.

Spending $500 on a haircut

*But the very hairs of your
head are all numbered.*

(Matthew 10:30)

Let no man or woman scoff at the fact that thou hast not a hair out of place, for those protestations come from those hindered by split ends, botched bangs, and shoddy home perms. It matters not that thou must run thine own hand constantly through thine own tresses, tossing them to and fro, for what thou hast is more than hair: it is a mane, majestic and full of body. Embrace thy dedication to thine one-named stylist and the extra care that goest into follicular maintenance, for thy locks deserve the best, even if that requires using a conditioning salve made from kangaroo placenta and guano.

Taking Casual Friday up
a notch by going pantless

Stand fast therefore in the liberty wherewith
Christ hath made us free, and be not
entangled again with the yoke of bondage.
(Galatians 5:1)

hrow off the constrictions of society and thine elastic-banded slacks, for thou hast read the employee handbook and there is no mention of a clothing requirement. And as thou embrace thy sartorial nothingness, realize that the look in thy fellow employees' eyes is not horrified shock, but jealousy, for thou hast gone further than anyone ever hath before. Thou shouldst be celebrated as an innovator and not treated as a pariah required to stay in thy cubicle while thine employers print out new employee handbooks. Remember, freedom, no matter how briefly tasted, is always satisfying.

Practicing thy stripper-pole dance lessons on the bar after a tray full of Jell-O shots

---

Who hath sent out the wild ass free? or who hath loosed the bands of the wild ass?

(Job 39:5)

After a couple margaritas, some rum, and a carafe of wine, thou hast come to the realization that there are more than two magnetic poles. It comes as no surprise that thou art ready to hang upon the plumbing, for the Almighty has a soft spot for bumping and grinding, and after another shot, thou shalt be ready to deliver on both counts. Just be certain to stuff thine inhibitions down with the dollar bills that shall soon be tucked into thine underwear elastic.

Augmenting thy chest
with fake breasts the size
of two mid-size animals

---

*Thy two breasts are like two young roes
that are twins, which feed among the lilies.*

(Song of Solomon 4:5)

---

hether or not thou pursueth a job in the adult entertainment industry, the Bible instructs that thou should not be deterred from the use of cosmetic surgery to improve thy self-image or income from tips. As far as the size of thy new twin enhancements, a good rule of thumb is to judge for thyself what is and what is not absolutely ridiculous, and then go up a cup size from that. Ignore those who would make claims of unforeseen back pain or an outlook of a pendulous future, for they are jealous and will surely want to have a feel after the surgery is completed.

Wearing a clown costume to rob a bank

⸺◦◦◦◦◦⸺

Abstain from all appearance of evil.
(1 Thessalonians 5:22)

⸺◦◦◦◦◦⸺

The Bible realizes that thou art not a bad person at heart, so why would thou dress like one when thou rob a bank? Turn frowns upside down with thy red nose and size-twenty shoes right before thou turn those smiles into grimaces of sheer terror when thou pull out thy gun. Whilst thou wait for the cashiers to hand over all the money, thou may want to tie balloon animals for the children. This gesture of kindness might also help to reduce thy sentence in the event that thou art caught. And seeing that thou art planning to make thine escape dressed like a clown, the possibility of apprehension is quite high.

Keeping a bedside chart rating
thy loved one's performances,
along with notes on the areas
in which they can improve

⟨≈⟩

Thou shouldest have smitten five or six times.
(2 Kings 13:19)

⟨≈⟩

ow better to improve thy love life than with a
dry-erase board and a pie chart? Nothing will
demonstrate love for thy partner like strong
organizational skills. Be honest with thy loved one about
areas that they need to improve on, pointing them out on
anatomical drawings if necessary. Set goals for thy beloved
and reward their efforts with stars that can be turned in
for ice cream and, if they collect enough, the opportunity
to take down the bedside chalkboard filled with details of
their many failings.

Menacing the neighborhood kids' street hockey game with thy van

A wise king scattereth the wicked, and bringeth the wheel over them.

(Proverbs 20:26)

Where are the parents of these children that line the streets? Should these tiny, non-winged angels not be indoors playing video games or harming each other? Instead, their parents have loosed them onto thy street, them and their constant, demonlike shrieking. Take action if thine attempts to sleep past noon hath been denied. Make a joyful noise as thou lay on thine horn as thy van comes skidding toward their game at unsafe speeds. Wave and smile as thou dragest one of their goals for miles. If questioned later by police, gasp at the thought that thou might have frightened little children, and tell them that the glory of God's sun was in thine eyes.

Smoking medical marijuana on the chance that thou may get sick in the future

---

Out of his nostrils goeth smoke, as out of a seething pot or caldron.

(Job 41:20)

Thy bravery in the face of potential illness should be truly inspiring to others. Doth the people around thee not realize that it is only a matter of time before thee art stricken with a terrible disease? Then they should questioneth not that thou hast started treatment early. And their speculation that there is a difference between medical marijuana and that which thou buyest from the guy around the corner is pure foolishness. Thou knowest the difference, and that should be enough for them and the police, who will be knocking on thy door within the hour.

Having thy boyfriend's old couch, posters, and T-shirt collection hauled away while he is at work

⁓∞⁓

Wherefore, as I live, saith the Lord God;
Surely, because thou hast defiled my
sanctuary with all thine detestable things,
and with all thy abominations, therefore will
I also diminish thee; neither shall mine eye
spare, neither will I have any pity.

(Ezekiel 5:11)

⁓∞⁓

Is the raggedy recliner that is a beloved treasure in thy boyfriend's eye an abomination against humanity in thine own? Follow the lessons of the Bible and purge thine home of the offending furniture and any miscellaneous objects that raise the bile of thy design sense. If no charity will take away thy beloved's nineteen-year-old sofa, perhaps thou canst break it down into trash-can-size chunks with an ax or chain saw. If the objects are resistant to breakage, there is always arson or faked robberies.

Selling a diet plan on late night television that is immensely successful because it is based on starvation

---

Ye shall not eat one day, nor two days, nor five days, neither ten days, nor twenty days.

(Numbers 11:19)

Hast thou led others to feel the burn as much as thou feel God's light? Clearly the Lord approves of thy vision to improve others with four simple payments of $19.99. It mattereth not that thy lesson is simple—what matters is that others consider it complex and that thou can repackage rice cakes at twice the price to go along with the simple lesson. Commend thyself for also discovering that packing "peanuts" make an excellent dietary supplement and also can be boxed without need for additional packaging.

Spending an entire party blocking others from the shrimp cocktail

---

These shall ye eat of all that are in the waters: whatsoever hath fins and scales in the waters, in the seas, and in the rivers, them shall ye eat.

(Leviticus 11:9)

If thou art invited to a party, take it upon thyself to arrive early and position thyself directly in front of the shrimp. Why? For some art fishers of men, some art fishers of fish, and for thee, free shrimp art thine elusive quarry. Surely human interaction is a small price to pay for the bounty of the sea. Ignore those who remark loudly that the appetizers were meant for more than one person; if they get any closer, thou can threaten them with thy crazy eyes and thy growing arsenal of cocktail toothpicks.

Never restraining thyself from saying, "I told thee so"

And I commanded you at that time all the things which ye should do.

(Deuteronomy 1:18)

There is no satisfaction in seeing someone thou love struggle through a terrible relationship or fall into an open manhole, unless thou hast warned them of those exact horrible events. Then the satisfaction is great. Remind them from this point until the day they die that not to heed thine advice is the highest folly. Imprint their failure upon them by mentioning their many missteps in public, along with highlighting thy starring role in their recovery.

Sneaking into a concert by telling the doorman that thou art just going to pop in to use the bathroom

―――――∞―――――

Let me pass through thy land: I will go along by the high way, I will neither turn unto the right hand nor to the left.

(Deuteronomy 2:27)

―――――∞―――――

How dareth those velvet ropes and large-boned men standeth between thee and the band thou desirest to see? Just because they have judged thee deficient in funds does not mean that they should have power over thee. If thou hast chosen to go to a rock show and prefer not to pay for it, make those flashlight-bearing demons part before thee like the Red Sea by telling them that thou must be on the list and to check under the name Smith. If this does not work, dance from one foot to the other, pointing in the general direction of thy bladder, and whimper to aid thee in gaining entrance to the Kingdom of Heavenly Music.

Sending thy children to live at "Camp Backyard" for the summer

---

Go say to them, Get you into your tents again.
(Deuteronomy 5:30)

Summer is an occasion to revel in the beauty of the Lord's creation and bathe in the rays of His sun. Sadly, it is the same time that schools have decided to loose thy children back upon thee. However, worry not, for a child's needs are simple and most of them can be met in thine own backyard. Sheltered within a WWI-era tent and with water from the hose, what more could they want besides the occasional hot dog? Worry not about the neighbors calling the authorities, for they are envious that thou thought of this first.

Demarcating thy personal space in a shared apartment with police tape and "Keep-Out" signs

Yet there shall be a space between you and it, about two thousand cubits by measure: come not near unto it, that ye may know the way by which ye must go: for ye have not passed this way heretofore.

(Joshua 3:4)

Set forth boundaries between thy possessions and thine housemate's, for it is better not to share than to have another use thy toothbrush. They might protest at the walls, physical and metaphorical, that thou hast set up between the two of ye. Just explain to them that the Almighty feels that sharing is overrated, for rarely art thou able to come out ahead in the equation. If thy roommate continueth to complain about such things as their half of the refrigerator being the freezer or their side of the bathroom not including a toilet, feel free to pull the curtain between ye shut.

*And he said, The Lord is my rock,
and my fortress, and my deliverer.*
(2 Samuel 22:2)

izza, particularly pepperoni pizza, is proof of the Divine, and delivery of pizza is a reflection of God's love for us. Therefore, thou must scoff at the delivery person who attempts to insinuate himself into this religious experience by holding out his empty hand. He is but a small cog in God's grand plan—a cog that forgot to bring pepper flakes. Remind him of his small participation in the Lord's divine machinations and, instead of a gratuity, reward him with a simple thumbs-up or a cheery smile.

Blaming thy weight gain on the busboy at last night's dinner

So I opened my mouth, and he caused me to eat that roll.

(Ezekiel 3:2)

D o not take the blame for any weight gain upon thyself. Pointing thy finger at thyself is too easy an answer. Instead, revisit the weeks and months previous, and pick the culprits from thy memories of previous meals. The busboy that brought thee that extra basket of rolls thou asked for? Guilty. The cashier who took thy ten-piece fried chicken order? Guilty. Thy grandmother and her cherry pie? That woman is guilty as sin. What art thou to do about deviltry such as this? Alas, nothing, for thou art afloat in a vast ocean of conspiracy meant to see that thou never wear a bathing suit again.

Flatly refusing to defend thy girlfriend's honor

But the men that went up with him said,
We be not able to go up against the people;
for they are stronger than we.

(Numbers 13:31)

As discretion is the better part of valor, so too is cowardice a vital part of survival. The Lord Almighty wants thee not only to survive, but also to remain uninjured. So if those larger than thee decide to disparage thy loved one's reputation, by all means, let them. In fact, if it will help thee not get hurt, maybe thou shouldst mock her as well. Of course, this shall turn thy girlfriend against thee, perhaps dangerously so. If she threatens thee with physical harm, thy best option is to lie on the ground and play dead. If she is anything like a bear, she might just leave thee alone.

Using a program of continual "constructive" criticism to enable thy boyfriend to improve himself

These things have I spoken unto you, that ye should not be offended.

(John 16:1)

Much like militarily achieved democracy-building, thou must break down thy new boyfriend before thou canst build him up to an image thou findest pleasing. It might take weeks, months, or years, but the final product will be worth it in the end. Indeed, if the only costs of this transformation are thy soul mate's long crying jags, they are a small price for him to pay for thine happiness. Take time to appreciate the journey of sleep deprivation and verbal abuse the two of ye are going through, and realize that the destination will be worth it. Surely, at some point in the future, perhaps thy sixtieth wedding anniversary, he will thank thee for what thou hast done to him.

Hiding from creditors
who would do thee harm

Verily I say unto thee, Thou shalt by no means come out thence, till thou hast paid the uttermost farthing.

(Matthew 5:26)

Hast thou lost a large amount of money that thou canst not pay back? Did the horses that thou placed money on to win, place, and show actually run last, lame, and disqualified? Are those that thou art indebted to planning to break thy fingers, one at a time? Then the Bible suggests that thou crawl upon the floor of thine home, keeping low to avoid the eyes of those who seek thee. Sitting in thy closet with the lights out is probably thy safest path. Whatsoever thou doest, answer not thy front door, even if is a floral delivery or a dancing banana, for these are both tricks of the creditors.

Accusing thy children of blasphemy when they claim to have never heard of Mick Jagger and Keith Richards

---

That this may be a sign among you, that when your children ask their fathers in time to come, saying, What mean ye by these stones?

(Joshua 4:6)

Thou hast not asked much of thy children, for thou art used to them disappointing thee. But surely they could take some interest in thy generation's music, for it was the last time anything sounded good. Do they not realize that their music is just noise, a nonsensical arrangement of bleeps, bloops, and hollas? Curse them for making light of thy collection of vinyl records or thine excitement at getting tickets to see a band that surprisingly did not die decades ago. If revenge is what thou desire, educate thy spawn by replacing their MP3 player with an 8-track.

Hanging up photos in thy cubicle from thy couples-only swingers vacation

And they were both naked, the man and his wife, and were not ashamed.

(Genesis 2:25)

Where doth Human Resources get the power to tell thee that thou should be ashamed of thy and thy significant other's bodies? The Lord created all in His image, and if HR has a problem with this, then they are obviously in league with Satan. Ignore the protestations of these tiny-minded demons and have thy photos blown up to poster size. Then all those who would speak against thee shall see the virtue of having no visible tan lines. Additionally, thou might want to get T-shirts emblazoned with thy vacation images to give away as presents to those who do not get to see enough of thee on a regular basis.

Escalating every minor restaurant mishap into an "I need to speak to thy manager" offense

---

We asked their names also, to certify thee, that we might write the names of the men that were the chief of them.

(Ezra 5:10)

Thou must accept that thy calling in life is to torment the service industry, so undertake thy task with vigor. God would be stricken to know that thou hast not had thy coffee refreshed or that thou hast had to ask twice for a third basket of tortilla chips. Therefore, let thy complaints of disappointment reverberate throughout the restaurant until they land upon the ears of the manager. Tell them that thou hast been dissatisfied and that thou dost not want to have to call the health board, but if thou hast to, thou shalt. Thine hard line will gain thee the respect of restaurant workers everywhere. They might try to poison thee, but they will still respect thee.

Altering thine appearance whilst on the run from the law

*And when I heard this thing, I rent
my garment and my mantle, and plucked
off the hair of my head and of my beard,
and sat down astonied.*

(Ezra 9:3)

Art thou desired and chased by those who would imprison thee? Hast thou just seen thy face accurately captured by an artist's rendering at the post office? Is a pair of sunglasses not enough to mask thine ankle-length hair, handlebar mustache, and neck tattoo of a mermaid with six-guns? Then it is time to take more drastic concealatory measures and denude thyself of thy life's previous trappings. Cut thine hair, shave, and cover thy mermaid with a very large anchor. And for God's sake, put on a shirt.

Informing thy loved one in the midst of coitus that it wouldn't hurt them to eat a salad every once in a while

---

Behold, I am pressed under you, as a cart is pressed that is full of sheaves.

(Amos 2:13)

If, during a time of carnal enjoyment, thy thoughts turn from the pleasure of the moment to the possibility of a broken pelvis, it is time to talk to thy loved one about their weight. As this is a sensitive topic, soften the remarks thou would normally make, avoiding comments such as "Dear Lord, I can't breathe!" or "Help me!" As soon as thy loved one gets off thee, speak gently about thine hopes and fears. If that does not work, tell them the bottom line is that unless they are to shed some pounds, their days on top are over.

Breaking up thy boyfriend's band by suggesting that his bandmates are limiting his potential by not giving him enough piccolo solos

Let us break their bands asunder,
and cast away their cords from us.

(Psalms 2:3)

Doth thy boyfriend's bandmates not realize the talent that lies within their midst? Why is thy loved one not standing at the center of the stage? Why doth he not have his own microphone? A lesson from the Bible teaches that thou must be the strength and urgency behind shattering the barriers of the band. If the band desireth to embrace piccolo-less mediocrity, by all means, let them. Fear not for thy boyfriend, for thou art setting him free. And perhaps he will let thee play bass in his next band.

Denying any knowledge of
thy former money manager's
accounting errors, his subsequent
escape to the Grand Caymans,
or the small islet thou hast
recently purchased

❦

*Who can understand his errors? cleanse
thou me from secret faults.*

(Psalms 19:12)

❦

It is best that thou knowest not the whereabouts
of thy money manager or the exact balance of thy
Swiss bank accounts, for the federal government
is desirous of both. As thou must tell them, how wert thou
to know that thine advisors had figured out a way for thee
not to pay taxes? Display thy shock and dismay at the fact
that the laws of commerce were not followed exactly.

Making thine yard the decorative center of the neighborhood with flamingos, gnomes, and an animatronic Santa

And this house, which is high, shall be an astonishment to every one that passeth by it; so that he shall say, Why hath the Lord done thus unto this land, and unto this house?

(2 Chronicles 7:21)

Yard decorations are a way for thee to leave a taste of thyself when thou art not around, much like the after-odor of a particularly strong perfume or sewage treatment plant. Place thy personal stamp on the public eye with decorations that say the most about thee, like thine holiday crèche with Santa as one of the three Magi. Ignore complaints that a crèche belongeth not on display in July, for those come from the voices of disbelievers. And if there were any question, know that there is no such thing as too many concrete cherubs.

Refusing to hold thy boyfriend's hands during the scary parts of horror movies

---

Withdraw thine hand far from me:
and let not thy dread make me afraid.

(Job 13:21)

The daily burden of thy boyfriend is great enough without needing to coddle his fears during a scary movie. Instead, derive some pleasure from his fear and take him to a horror movie to watch him squirm, his growing terror a wonderful side dish to the eight-dollar popcorn he bought thee. Pull thine hand away and allow him to cower behind his entwined fingers. Let "yes" be thine answer to all of his "Can I look now?" inquiries, no matter how much cinematic carnage is about to commence. The Bible does not care for scaredy cats or cowardly men, and neither shouldst thou.

Wearing a wire to thy friend's house in an effort to reduce thine own prison sentence

---

Thy own mouth condemneth thee, and not I:
yea, thine own lips testify against thee.
(Job 15:6)

In the question of thee versus them, the Bible teaches that there is only one, obvious choice. So make sure that thy friends speaketh clearly into the flower in thy lapel as the government agent instructed thee, and don't fidget with thy microphone tie or take off the top hat with the camera in it. Think not of thyself as a stool pigeon; instead think of thyself as a freckle on the long arm of justice with a golden future in the Witness Protection Program. If thou art looking for a great new name, consider Snake, Tiger, or Raven.

Sitting on thy brother's head until he agrees to loan thee his car

And so, after he had patiently endured, he obtained the promise.

(Hebrews 6:15)

Thy violence toward thine own brother doth not signify a lack of love. Nay, it is just how decisions are made between ye. If he says no to any of thy requests, thou just pummel him until that answer becometh yes. If he holdeth staunchly to his refusal, ask of him, "Why dost thou keep hitting thyself?" as thou batter him about the head with his own hand. Eventually ye two will come to a satisfying agreement. As soon as he stops hitting himself.

Bulking up for winter, or perhaps a professional sumo career, with a diet of bacon-wrapped bacon

~~~

Thou art weighed in the balances,
and art found wanting.

(Daniel 5:27)

~~~

Hast thou decided to put some meat on thy bones? Know that God's love for thee grows along with thy waistband and that thou can best celebrate His abundance by eating a large portion of it. Whatever the reason for thy weight gain, make sure thou hast fun with it. For example, if thou hast already consumed 300% of thy Recommended Daily Allowance of saturated fat, see if thou canst beat 350%. For movie night, skip the popcorn and eat a stick of butter. Just remember to keep eating, because despite how much thou might weigh, the Lord will always be left wanting more.

Bringing thine "A" game to the recreation-league soccer game

Wherefore that field was called,
The field of blood, unto this day.

(Matthew 27:8)

Dost thou feel the eyes of the opposing team as thou calls upon the Lord to strike them down beneath thy cleats? Truly, thou art the backbone of thy team and Almighty's tool. If not for thee, who would bring the orange slices and loudly debate every referee call? Pity others, for what they consider but recreation is actually a life-and-death struggle against evil. Therefore take no notice of the accumulated yellow cards and continue to give 110%, for thine understanding of percentages is rudimentary at best.

Discovering thy rash was caused not by thy partner's indiscretions but thine own

---

It is more blessed to give than to receive.
(Acts 20:35)

Knowing that thy lover did not cheat soothes th heart as much as thy shared rash irritates th groin and upper-thigh area. Blame not thine ow wandering loins, for it was but a minor indiscretion tha can be cleared up with a small course of antibiotics. To caln the heart of thy nearest and dearest, blame thy matchin; ailments on a gas station bathroom, the bite of a strang animal, or an Act of God.

Adding excitement and spectacular meltdowns to any evening by giving thy friends' children candy corn and jawbreakers

---

They reel to and fro, and stagger like a drunken man, and are at their wit's end.

(Psalms 107: 27)

Art thou childless? Dost thou prefer it that way? Dost thou find that visiting friends who have been "blessed" with offspring is equivalent to painful torture, such as being drawn and quartered? For the totless, children are like cats who are most attracted to those who are allergic to them. Instead of letting them hang off thee like thou art a piece of playground equipment, ply the young with sugary sweets. Then stand back and watch as the precious little jewels careen, screaming from room to room like bottle rockets. Then, after their parents pry their tiny fingernails from the ceiling, it is off to bed with them and time for adult fun to begin.

Waking up on thy bathroom floor with the worst hangover in the world

For the great day of his wrath is come; and who shall be able to stand?

(Revelation 6:17)

ast thou awakened on the bathroom floor? Is the only relief to thy pain achieved from placing thy forehead against the cold tiles? Dost thy tongue taste like the sole of a shoe? Take pride in the damage done to thyself by heroic amounts of alcohol, for it is as if thou took on one of God's curses by thyself and survived, though severely hampered and possibly self-soiled. Legions of frogs and locusts and lamb's blood on doorways would be an improvement to that which vexes thee.

Sucker punching the guy who just called thee gutless

It is hard for thee to kick against the pricks.
(Acts 9:5)

There will always be a Goliath to thy David, a bully who will taunt thee. Unfortunately, because sling-based assaults are no longer legally permissible, thou must find another way to strike at thine enemy. As with most tormentors, he is expecting thee to kick back at him or punch him in the face. It is at this point that he will break thee over his leg like a pretzel stick. That is why thou must avoid frontal attacks and instead jump on his back like a rabid lemur to exact any revenge that requires exacting. Certainly at some point in the evening, he shall be able to peel thee off and will undoubtedly give thee a coach-class ticket to a world of pain, but wasn't thy revenge, though short-lived and negligible, worth it?

Telling thy boyfriend that thou dost not feel like making out due to the large pimple on his nose

---

A time to cast away stones, and a time to gather stones together; a time to embrace, and a time to refrain from embracing.

(Ecclesiastes 3:5)

Thy boyfriend might feel as though thou hast forsaken him, but the Bible teaches that there is a thin line between pity and an insane disregard for hygiene displayed by loved ones. If thy lover feels like an oily-faced sinner, it is thy job to remind him of this truth. Let reason with just a touch of irrationality be thy guide as thou request that he touch nothing in thine house, including thy person. Is this cruel? Nay, for thy callousness towards him is balanced by thy compassion for thyself. If he insists on sticking around, hold a towel over thy mouth and try to refrain from making gagging sounds.

Breaking up thy gay friend's relationship for the betterment of thy social life

─────────────○○○─────────────

I tell you, in that night there shall be two men in one bed; the one shall be taken, and the other shall be left.

(Luke 17:34)

─────────────○○○─────────────

Pray tell, why doth thy friend abide with such an intolerable partner? Truly, if two men are to share the same bedchamber, it matters not to thee. It is just that thy friend's lover cannot eat a meal without commenting negatively on everything from the appetizer to the restaurant's choice of artificial sweetener. The Bible mandates that thou must think of some artifice to separate the couple—possibly a white lie or a faked kidnapping—and then explain to thy friend that thou thinkest it would be best if he were to sever his obviously poisonous relationship. Verily, it would make thy Sunday brunch plans much easier.

Cloning thyself to make the world a better place

*Be fruitful, and multiply,
and replenish the earth.*

(Genesis 1:28)

Hast thou ever wondered what the Earth would do without thee? The Bible teaches that God loves thee so much he'd love to have two of thee. Moreover, identical clones would be great fun at parties and reunions, and convenient if thou ever needed a replacement liver. Take note that thou shouldst be wary of any goateed clones, for they are evil and will undoubtedly work to destroy thee, unless thou hast a goatee, in which case thou art evil and will probably enjoy their company.

Assuring thine enemy that thy dog's growl is just his way of saying hello

❮❮❮❮❮

That thy foot may be dipped in the blood of thine enemies, and the tongue of thy dogs in the same.

(Psalms 68:23)

❮❮❮❮❮

Doth thy foe want to pet thy dog? By all means, allow them to put their hand near thy beast's slavering jaws. Thou made that same mistake and now thou cannot grip a tennis ball or sleep with the bedroom door unlocked. Thank the Lord for blessing thee with a furry vehicle of undirected ferocity; just make sure thou feign shock when blood is inevitably spilled.

Taking thy beauty regimen to the next level with a full-body depilatory

---

Therefore God dealt well with the midwives: and the people multiplied, and waxed very mighty.

(Exodus 1:20)

All people are beautiful in the eyes of the Lord, but even He would agree that there are some who are rather on the hirsute side. In any event, while the Almighty is omniscient, He probably farms out the follicle department to one of His lesser angels, so feel no regret if thou decide to pull the no-hair trigger. The Bible teaches that there is nothing wrong with having somebody slather thy body with wax and then rip it up like old carpet. Embrace the transformation from welcome mat to naked as the day thou were born. Beware, however, as it is just going to grow back thicker and darker.

Opening a petting zoo featuring thine exotic reptile collection

For every kind of beasts, and of birds, and of serpents, and of things in the sea, is tamed, and hath been tamed of mankind.

(James 3:7)

The Lord has blessed humanity with dominion over all the creatures of the Earth, from snakes that spit poison to lizards that shoot blood from their eyes. And luckily for the curious, thou hast gathered these two, and other fascinatingly volatile reptiles, into one roadside, chicken-wired enclosure. What better way for people to learn about venomous reptiles than direct contact? Educate thy visitors by explaining that a cobra is as scared of them as they of it, and not to let its continued lunging toward their ankles fool them. Also, tell them they can find antivenin in thy gift shop, right next to the refrigerator magnets.

Driving thy rental car
to its untimely death

And the work of the wheels was like the work of a chariot wheel: their axletrees, and their naves, and their felloes, and their spokes, were all molten.

(1 Kings 7:33)

A ccidents happen, and, the rental company should realize, that they happen to thee more often than not. Is it thy fault that thou turned a minivan into a midsize convertible? Nay, thou art innocent in all of this. It is a matter of public knowledge that thou can barely drive. Most would know not to lend thee a motor vehicle or, for that matter, anything sharp. Just as thou would not hand a box of dynamite to a monkey with a match, neither should anyone be giving thee the opportunity to operate an automobile.

Forgetting to mention Montezuma's revenge to thine annoying housemate when suggesting vacation destinations

---

And this water that causeth the curse shall go into thy bowels, to make thy belly to swell, and thy thigh to rot: And the woman shall say, Amen, amen.

(Numbers 5:22)

Is thy soon-to-be-on-vacation roommate prancing about in her bikini? Maybe if she weren't so sinfully prideful, thou might give her a little information about the perils bacteria-wise of the vacation spot thou suggested to her. Didst thou stifle a laugh when she asked if she'd need immunizations? Consider thyself a teacher and she the student who will need some extra help. It will be fun for ye to discuss the many errors of her ways when she gets home.

Building a robot to exact revenge upon all those who ever laughed at thee

Then I would know the truth of the fourth beast, which was diverse from all the others, exceeding dreadful, whose teeth were of iron, and his nails of brass; which devoured, brake in pieces, and stamped the residue with his feet.

(Daniel 7:19)

Vengeance is all thine, sayeth the Lord, especially if thou hast the ability to build a robot. Thou art not stupid, thou hast seen the movies and thou know that one day in the future robots will kill everybody. Why not start early on the robo-pocalypse by ordering plans for thine own mechanical servant from the back of a magazine? Thou know that thou shalt never finish it, for, the Lord knows, thou never finish anything, but just the idea that thy creation is only 700 man-hours and a lawn mower engine away will surely chill the hearts of thine enemies.

Claiming that thy trick knee is the only thing stopping thee from carrying thy new bride across the threshold

---

How can I myself alone bear your cumbrance, and your burden, and your strife?

(Deuteronomy 1:12)

Marriage is a burden and there is no reason to add more to thy load, especially on the first night. Maybe thou can tip the bellboy to carry thy new wife through the doorway whilst thou valiantly hold the door open, or maybe he can just roll her through on the luggage cart. To be fair to thy new partner in life, if thou art going to start disappointing her, it is right to do it from the beginning and not surprise her in a month or so. This might also be a good time to clip thy toenails on the bed.

Screaming "In thy face, losers!"
at the approximately 40,000
people who are cheering
for the other team

———◇◇◇———

*I will not be afraid of ten thousands
of people, that have set themselves
against me round about.*

(Psalms 3:6)

———◇◇◇———

Find great comfort in the knowledge that, when it comes to team sports, the Lord has taken thy side, for the Lord loves winners. For this reason, thou art absolutely right to find comfort in the distress of opposing fans. Why would thou not harangue their choice to cheer for a team that cannot do anything correctly? Celebrate thy love for the Lord by painting thy face in the colors of the victor and shouting at even the most minor victories, such as coin flips and time-outs. Do call-and-response cheers by thyself. Buy a horn that sounds like a mournful goat and blow into it constantly, as if thou were bringing down the walls of Jericho.

Purchasing a Rolls-Royce as thy ministerial-work car

*And whatsoever shall seem good
to thee, and to thy brethren, to do with
the rest of the silver and the gold, that
do after the will of your God.*

(Ezra 7:18)

Much of ministering is travel, whether it be to the bank to make deposits or to parishioners' homes to pick up checks. On rare occasions thou must even visit the sick and/or elderly. Remind thyself that thou art doing the Lord's work—why would He want thee to suffer for thy goodness? To be sure, God wants thee, nay, needs thee to have heated seats and tiny windshield wipers for thine headlights. However, to dispel any jealousy in thy congregation over the obvious fact that the Almighty loves thee the most, tell them that the car was an anonymous donation.

Indulging in very public displays of affection with thy loved one

~~~

One is so near to another, that no air can come between them.

(Job 41:16)

~~~

Let not the eyes of a stranger arrest thee from showing affection to thy loved one, no matter if there are only three of thee in the elevator. Revel in thy lover's complete lack of inhibitions and display thine affection by licking the side of her head and repeatedly dry-humping her leg. Ignore the gagging protestations of thy witness, for groping thy lover in public is surely blessed by the Lord.

Refusing to allow others to dissuade thee from test-driving thy "rocket car"

To subvert a man in his cause,
the Lord approveth not.

(Lamentations 3:36)

It is unfortunate that there will always be those who will try to shake thee from thy dreams. These naysayers may cry science or "sanity" as reasons for thee not to fly thy lawn chair balloon or fill thy gas tank with a mix of gasoline and fireworks, but the root of their complaints is just envy at the imaginative ways thou art endangering thine own life. God Almighty instructs thee to free thyself of their imposed reason by saying that thou shalt consider their criticism and then, as they smugly claim sanity has won, jumping into thy rocket car and blasting off. Thy courage and their singed eyebrows will be remembered for a lifetime.

Refusing to wear the sweater
thy girlfriend knitted thee

◇◇◇

And if thou deal thus with me, kill me, I pray
thee, out of hand, if I have found favour in
thy sight; and let me not see my wretchedness.
(Numbers 11:15)

◇◇◇

Dost wearing the sweater that thy girlfriend knitted thee make it seem as if thou art on thy way to a circus audition? Dost thou have a sartorial reputation to maintain, no matter how meager? Certainly, as the Bible teaches, ending thy life would put a conclusion to thy wardrobe troubles, but there is another way to get out of that synthetic-fibered atrocity without offending thy loved one. Tell her that thou hast been robbed, the thief bedazzled by thy sweater of many colors. If she offereth to knit thee another, tell her that the memories associated with the original are too painful for thy sorrowful heart.

Claiming that the deck
of cards that fell out of thy
sleeve was in no way meant
to affect the poker game

---

*And both these kings' hearts shall be to do
mischief, and they shall speak lies at one
table; but it shall not prosper: for yet the
end shall be at the time appointed.*

(Daniel 11:27)

---

hy art thou beleaguered by others for thine
attempt to bring some order to a game of
chance? Just because thou hast figured out a
better way to play the game does not mean that thou hast
cheated others or that thou expected to profit from it. And
even if thou didst profit from it, thy true reward is the
natural evolution of the game. Why shouldst thou take
blame for being ahead of the thought curve? And if thy
fellow players cannot appreciate innovation such as thine,
take thine extra deck of cards and thy X-ray spectacles and
back swiftly out of the room, for it is time for thee to go.

Saving on the costs of home-building materials by using papier-mâché and cardboard

---

And they said one to another, Go to, let us make brick, and burn them thoroughly. And they had brick for stone, and slime had they for morter.

(Genesis 11:3)

The Bible says that appearances can be deceiving, which works for thee because the house thou hast just finished looks great. Hopefully the new owners will not hear the creaking or see the electrical outlets catch fire before thou hast driven out of sight. Regardless, they have little to complain about, for thou didst pass part of the savings on to them, when thou bought their wonderful hot tub. There is no reason that they need to know that thou picked it up for half-price at a crime scene.

Berating thy neighborhood barista when thy coffee is not up to par

---

So then because thou art lukewarm, and neither cold nor hot, I will spue thee out of my mouth.

(Revelation 3:16)

Hath those in the employ of the local coffee shop attempted to give thee coffee that last dripped hours ago? Display thy dissatisfaction by spitting out the offending liquid and making choking noises. Fall to thy knees and malignest those who would feed thee this insipid brew. Implore God to strike them down, for thou hast been poisoned. Accept thy new free coffee without comment.

Telling thy book club
thou read the book when thou only watched the movie

And no man in heaven, nor in earth, neither under the earth, was able to open the book, neither to look thereon.

(Revelation 5:3)

The only good book is the Good Book, and truly even that is better on tape. It is no secret that reading is an assault on the senses, besieging thy mind with new ideas and causing eye trauma. It is stimulation of the worst sort and just because thou hast joined a book club for the camaraderie and free snacks does not mean thou shouldst read. Instead, rent movies of the books or movies that have titles that are similar to the books. When asked what thou thought of the book, just eat another cookie and mumble.

Canceling the stripper for thy fiancé's bachelor party

That no flesh should glory in his presence.

(1 Corinthians 1:29)

Who doth thy fiancé think he is? Whilst thou hast spent months consulting with florists, organists, and priests in order to make thy wedding the most special of days, he and his cohorts have hired a whore to wiggle her nether regions in their faces. This, the Bible teaches, will not do. Speak to thy beloved's friends and explain to them that if this morally loose woman dances before them, it will be the last time they are able to walk without noticeable limps. Suggest that if they are in need of excitement, they can go drive go-carts or use the batting cages.

Kicking thine one-night stand out of the house before he has the opportunity to find his pants

---

As soon as the morning was light, the men were sent away, they and their asses.

(Genesis 44:3)

Fret not if thou awaken only to send thy previous night's bedmate out of thy chamber in shame. Or that he was still looking for articles of clothing when thou shoved him out the doorway. Surely he knew that thy love was to be short-lived when thou told him that thou had no interest in his name, or when thou blindfolded him and spun him three times before bringing him home.

Hypnotizing thy friend to cluck like a chicken

Now therefore, my son, obey my voice according to that which I command thee.

(Genesis 27:8)

Hast thou agreed to help a friend quit smoking? Truly, that is a noble gesture and one that thou should be proud of, but is there anything thou can get out of the experience? While thou art altering thy friend's brain, thou might as well make some improvements. Hast thou considered how much fun it would be to have a zombielike companion to do thy bidding or a companion who will bark like a dog at the snap of thy fingers? With thy friend's unconscious devotion and thy nonexistent conscience, there will be no end to the fun.

Enjoying some strenuous locker-room shenanigans with the guys

---

His hand will be against every man,
and every man's hand against him.

(Genesis 16:12)

If there is one thing that the Bible appreciates, it is the purity of horseplay among men. There is something about the sight of undressed, athletic males that arouses the idea of roughhousing amongst them. Therefore, let go thy inhibitions and thy towel as thou engage in playful jostling and drink in the intoxicating sheen of sweat on muscular shoulders.

Starting mean rumors about those who art more successful than thou

---

Thine eyes are upon the haughty, that thou mayest bring them down.

(2 Samuel 22:28)

A lot of people may believe they're superior to thee, whether they be smarter, faster, or more successful in every field of endeavor. They may even have proof of their accomplishments in the form of medals, advanced degrees, and novelty "World's Best" trophies, but thou shouldst not let that stop thee from trying to knock these false idols off their unholy pedestals. Feel free to employ unflattering caricatures and unfounded rumors. Remember: Thou art not just undermining others—thou art also building thyself up, which is saintly indeed.

Drinking to excess, then having a shot of tequila

Drink no longer water, but use a little wine for thy stomach's sake.

(1 Timothy 5:23)

The Bible is full of divine, sage medical advice. Thy body does not just need alcohol, it is desperately crying out for it. What art thou waiting for? Get thee down to the liquor store and do something good unto thy body. It should be noted that as a Biblical cubit is the distance between one's thumb and elbow, a "little wine" is actually the modern-day equivalent of one-and-a-half bottles of merlot; a giant snifter of various coconut rums, tropical juices, and novelty straws; or a case of inexpensive canned beer. Let thy hangover be thy halo.

Threatening thy neighbor after he has the rusted car in thy front yard removed

---

Cursed be he that removeth his neighbour's landmark. And all the people shall say, Amen.
(Deuteronomy 27:17)

Do not stay thy verbal sword from whosoever took the vehicle that sat on thy lawn for a decade and was any day to be restored to its original beauty. The Lord understands that thy neighbor must feel the wrath of thine words, no matter how much thou sputterest in thy rage. Let thy betrayer senseth the cold of thy stony gaze, no matter when ye make eye contact, whether they driveth past thine house at noon or looketh out at their lawn in the predawn hours. If need be, drive doughnuts on his lawn and then suggest it was the work of local hooligans.

Employing a workforce that has yet to lose its baby teeth

It is good for a man that he bear the yoke in his youth.

(Lamentations 3:27)

Whether it is raking leaves, painting fences, or sewing in a cramped hotbox of a warehouse space for eighteen hours at a time, the Bible commands that labor is good for children. The sweat of their tiny brows provides a great life lesson for them, plus they tend to recover much more quickly from industrial accidents. Unfortunately, due to government interference, actually putting a yoke on the little cherubs (strictly for behavioral training) is illegal in forty-eight states, hence creating an additional reason to open thy workhouse in Mississippi or New Hampshire.

Making friends through boot licking and groveling

Speak that which is good.

(1 Kings 22:13)

he Bible commands that thou must hold those with power over thee in the greatest esteem and that thou must make thine admiration clear to all. Everybody likes their praises sung, especially employers, celebrities, and anybody with more money than thee. These people particularly like it when thou rephrase something that they have just said and repeat it to them. Continual, undiluted reverence shall result in a rapid rise through the ranks of whatever organization thou art involved with; however, be prepared to temper thine agreeability in front of grand juries and congressional hearings if things seem like they are going to Hell.

---◇◇◇---

*But many that are first shall be
last; and the last shall be first.*
(Matthew 19:30)

---◇◇◇---

If the Lord our God wanted the pious to wait in line at the bank, the Department of Motor Vehicles, or a family funeral, then He would not have blessed thee with the ability to create distractions such as fake heart attacks, trash-can fires, or the ever-popular, "Hey, look, a baby wolf!" It is, therefore, deeply sinful not even to fake a small seizure, especially if the line be long and the day be short.

Roughly gratifying thyself in the privacy of thy bedroom

And thou shalt have a paddle upon thy weapon; and it shall be, when thou wilt ease thyself abroad, thou shalt dig therewith, and shalt turn back and cover that which cometh from thee.

(Deuteronomy 23:13)

Modern life is fraught with pressures and there is nothing sinful about pleasuring thyself to relieve stress, perhaps while flipping through the latest underwear catalogs or watching the local weatherperson. However, sometimes time constraints, or the sound of approaching footsteps, require that this self-pleasure be practiced a bit more energetically. The Good Book teaches that there is no shame in meeting one's own physical needs vigorously, unless thy mother walketh in during thine erotic flagellation, in which case shame shall forever be thine, especially if she mentions it in her Christmas letter.

Stealing paper clips and reams of paper from thine employer

Thou shalt not oppress a hired servant that is poor and needy.

(Deuteronomy 24:14)

ake faith in the knowledge that the Bible understands how hard thou labor, day in and day out. Though thou may have a 401k and dental, oppression hangs over thee like fluorescent lighting. Rise up against thy despot/employer by surfing the Internet for shoe bargains and pasting magazine eyes into glasses frames (to simulate consciousness during meditative naps). Let thy righteousness rail against workplace tyranny with the frequent liberation of staplers, toilet paper, and color photocopiers. Most importantly, make no contributions to the coffee fund but do drink the coffee.

Helping speed the evolution of five-legged frogs by pouring industrial chemicals into the lake

*The depths have covered them:
they sank into the bottom as a stone.*

(Exodus 15:5)

Hast thou been tasked with the discarding of environmental pollutants? Dost thou feel not like driving out to a hazardous waste facility? In that case, the Bible teaches that any local body of water would be ideal for deep-sixing thy problems, as water covers so much, including seven-tenths of the Earth, Atlantis, and evidence of past mistakes. Take thy transgressions and cast them upon the waters. Poke holes in thy troubles to help them sink.

Informing a classroom full of children that, due to their parents' reluctance to purchase enough band candy, Christmas has been canceled

---

The Lord hath been sore displeased with your fathers.

(Zechariah 1:2)

All have witnessed the spectacular meltdowns of children that involve wailing, rending and/or removal of clothing, and throwing themselves to the ground. The Bible suggests that thou make use of this misbehavior as even the hardiest adult will agree to anything to stop their child from running in a circle, screeching, "Don't touch me!" in a public place. Win children over to thine opinion with cookies—the gold standard for the young—as well as balloons and talk of bunny rabbits. Inform them that, in fact, their parents are "meanies" for disagreeing with thy point of view and then set them upon the people who bore them as tiny emotional time bombs.

Sharing thine exemplary musical tastes with all those in range of thy car stereo and subwoofer

---

*Behold their sitting down, and
their rising up; I am their musick.*
(Lamentations 3:63)

Music soothes the soul, so it is selfish of thee to not share thy listening preferences with those within a mile of thy car. Some unsuspecting listeners will interpret the thumping of thy bass to be a mild earthquake, but they will soon realize that this sound is completely man-made and God-approved when the higher ranges begin to shatter glassware. As for thy choice of what selections to play, it does not particularly matter, for at volumes such as these, it is all rather deafening.

Yelling out thy car window at hitchhiking hippies

And thou, son of man, take thee a sharp knife, take thee a barber's razor, and cause it to pass upon thine head and upon thy beard: then take thee balances to weighe, and divide the hair.

(Ezekiel 5:1)

We are all God's children, though hippies are more like His stepchildren. Why else would the Almighty damn them to a life of distracting, swaying dances and incense that does not, in fact, hide smells but only makes them worse? Worry not, then, if thou decide to deride them and their sense of fashion, for it is clear that they are not in the Lord's favor as thou art. That thou wouldst even take notice of these societal outcasts is a sign of thy righteousness, even if thou art only telling them to cut their hair.

Playing dodgeball to win against kindergartners

And they shall fight against thee; but they shall not prevail against thee; for I am with thee, saith the Lord, to deliver thee.

(Jeremiah 1:19)

Is a victory any less sweet because thou hast achieved it against those who are two feet shorter than thee and five years old? Nay, for the Lord is on thy side, and he would see those who stand against thee trampled beneath thy feet or felled by a red rubber ball coming from thine hand like a cannon shot. If the sight of teary children brings sympathy to thine heart, remember that thou art teaching them a life lesson that will endureth long after their ball-shaped welts fade.

Basing major life decisions on dart games and fortune cookies

Despise not prophesyings.
(1 Thessalonians 5:20)

Naysayers will decry thy use of prophecy to decide thy future, but thanks to a fortune cookie, thou knew they would say that. The Bible embraces the fact that thou hast discovered that true direction in life comes only after a pleasant meal of steamed dumplings and pork fried rice. Indeed, crack open that odd-tasting cookie and decipher thy future, whether it be great fortune, a long trip, or a pleasant surprise. Though if it seems that thou might have accidentally gotten another diner's fortune, thou art allowed to trade with them. Also, the Almighty would like thee to add the words "in bed" to each of thy fortunes, for it brings much joy to the Heavenly Host.

Behaving inappropriately when thou see a celebrity

When they saw the star, they rejoiced with exceeding great joy

(Matthew 2:10)

If the performances of television and movie actors touch thee, why should thou not return the favor when thou glimpse them in public? Because of their exposure, it might feel as if thou already know them and this notion is correct according to the Good Book. So ignore the wishes and forearm shivers of their 300-pound bodyguards and approach the famous as one would meet an old friend, at full speed and shouting. Allow nothing less than the signing of thy bared chest and a photo that captures the moment: the celebrity acting terrified, his bodyguard announcing a "code red" into his walkie-talkie, and thee and thy beatific smile.

Organizing a book burning
for thy rival's new book

---

*For it is written, I will destroy the wisdom
of the wise, and will bring to nothing
the understanding of the prudent.*

(1 Corinthians 1:19)

Hast thou decided on a book's lack of literary value solely on thy disdain for its author? Good for thee! Thou shalt use poetic license to inflame thy community against thine enemy's literary atrocity. Censor not thy words as thou educate the local populace's lesser lights on the merits of fiery destruction. Hath not anyone read the book in question? So much the better, for knowledge only slows progress. Happily, nothing is as simple as a book burning, for all thou needest are fire and the phone number of the fire department when the aforementioned literary bonfire gets out of control. On a final note, this might be a good time to mention that this book hath been printed on fireproof parchment.

Reverend Hellenback is the founder and sole stockholder of the Universal Church of Sanctioned Indulgence. A graduate of a Bible college in eastern Pennsylvania that is either no longer accredited or never actually existed, Hellenback lives in Missouri with twelve Irish setters named after the Apostles. Apparently, Judas is a biter.

Dave Johnston is a graduate of Haverford College. Mr. Johnston claims that the only contact he had with Reverend Hellenback was late-night phone calls for which he was forced to pay. Mr. Johnston professes his love for all religions, no matter how much they contradict themselves. He suggests anyone angered by this book take their concerns to the aforementioned Reverend Hellenback.

INDEX

EDITOR: Kristin Mehus-Roe

DESIGNERS: Samantha Caplan, Kasey Free

PRODUCTION COORDINATORS: Shirley Woo, Diane Ross

COPYRIGHT © 2008 DAVE JOHNSTON

Abrams Image books are available at special discounts when purchased in quantity for premiums and promotions as well as fundraising or educational use. Special editions can also be created to specification. For details, contact specialmarkets@hnabooks.com or the address below.

HNA ▮▮▮▮▮
harry n. abrams, inc.
a subsidiary of La Martinière Groupe

115 West 18th Street
New York, N Y 10011
www.hnabooks.com

Printed and bound in China
10 9 8 7 6 5 4 3 2 1

Library of Congress Cataloging-in-Publication Data

Johnston, Dave, 1970-
Make the Bible Work for You! / by Dave Johnston.
p. cm.
"Reverend Hellenback"—Cover.
ISBN 978-0-8109-7102-8
1. Bible—Humor. I. Title.

PN6231.B45H45 2008

818'.602—dc22

2008004794